THE LAST DAYS
OF
SOUTHERN STEAM

FROM THE BILL REED
COLLECTION

THE LAST DAYS

≋ OF ≋

SOUTHERN STEAM

FROM THE BILL REED COLLECTION

In Full Colour

PETER TUFFREY

FONTHILL

Eastleigh Shed 34021

Bulleid 'West Country' Pacific no. 34021 *Dartmoor* shines in the sunlight at Eastleigh shed. One of two class members built in January 1946, no. 34021 was rebuilt in January 1958 along with no. 34012 *Launceston*. The cost of transforming *Dartmoor* was quite high, £10,464, whereas the other engines rebuilt around this time had approximately £8,500 spent on the process; the price for no. 34012 was the lowest at £7,646.

Fonthill Media Limited
Fonthill Media LLC
www.fonthillmedia.com
office@fonthillmedia.com

First published 2016

ISBN 978-1-78155-489-0

Printed in the UK

Contents

Halwill Station 30338
Drummond 'T9' locomotive no. 30338 is at the head of a train which has stopped at Halwill station before travelling onwards towards Exeter at the end of August 1960. The engine was the last member of the class to be sent into traffic from Nine Elms Works during October 1901. At this time an eight-wheel tender was provided, but no. 30338 had to wait until January 1923 to be equipped with a superheater. At the time of this picture the locomotive was working from Exmouth Junction and would be subsequently withdrawn from the depot in April 1961.

Page Two : Bournemouth Shed 30865
A problem appears to have occurred with Bournemouth shed's turntable, or with a locomotive using the equipment, requiring the warning flags and signals to be brought out. 'Lord Nelson' no. 30865 *Sir John Hawkins* waits for the issue to be resolved in April 1958. The locomotive was the final member of the class to be completed at Eastleigh Works in November 1929 and was initially to be named 'Viscount Jellicoe', First Sea Lord from 1916 to December 1917. But this idea was dropped in favour of Sir John Hawkins, who was a prominent figure in Elizabethan naval affairs and Vice Admiral when the Spanish Armada was defeated in 1588.

Introduction

At 81 years of age, life-long Nottingham resident Bill Reed has got an insatiable appetite for photographing locomotives. He has travelled all over the world to witness the numerous types, both steam and diesel, at work in service and preservation. These voyages have taken Bill to America, Canada, wide swathes of Europe and he even peeked behind the 'Iron Curtain', when still in existence.

Bill, while capturing images of diesels, is a 'steam man' at heart and can trace this fondness to early childhood. A local journey to visit his aunt was taken by Sentinel steam railcar and he would marvel at two of the regulars operating the service - no. 5192 *Rising Sun* and no. 51908 *Expedition*. By the age of ten, Bill had acquired his first *ABC of British Locomotives* by Ian Allan. This allowed him to recognise the many classes in operation on the ex-Great Central line which ran at the bottom of his father's allotment and where Bill spent many hours, doing little work, during his formative years.

Whereas some people are unsure of their vocation, Bill had his mind set on pursuing a career on the railways. The only vacancy he could find, however, was as a messenger lad at Nottingham Victoria station. On a platform here, one day during his lunch break, Bill encountered local photographer Freddie Guildford. He encouraged the young man to take pictures of locomotives and offered to impart his knowledge of developing film, which the junior enthusiast was only too happy to accept. Bill's camera around this time was a Kodak 127 with perforated bellows.

Bill finally obtained a job with locomotives, albeit as a cleaner, in early 1950 when he joined the staff of Nottingham depot starting on the road to becoming a driver, which was his ultimate ambition. However, Bill's joy at starting his new role was short lived as National Service recruited him and the next few years were spent with the Royal Corps of Signals in Singapore. One of the tasks given Bill was performing guard duty at the military hospital and this was one of the more enjoyable times, he says, as the post allowed him to watch the trains passing on the line to Kuala Lumpur.

British Railways employed Bill as a fireman, again at Nottingham, when demobbed in 1955 and at this time he purchased an Agfa Super Isolette camera. This was used to take pictures, not only of the motive power in the Nottingham area, but locomotives in operation around the country. Bill travelled extensively during the late 1950s and early 1960s capturing the new and the old engines at work in the respective regions of B.R. During this time Bill acquired a Canon 35 mm colour camera and also used a Bolex 8 mm cine camera.

This album consists of over 170 colour photographs taken in the Southern Region of B.R., which was formerly the lines constituting the Southern Railway. Bill took the pictures between 1958 and 1967 during a number of visits to stations, sheds and areas offering attractive vantage points of locomotives. He has managed to capture representatives from Bulleid's reign as Chief Mechanical Engineer of the Southern in the 'Q1' Class 0-6-0s, 'Merchant Navy' Pacifics and the numerous 'Light' Pacifics. His predecessor Richard Maunsell's 'N' Class 2-6-0s are well represented alongside examples of the 'Schools' Class, 'Lord Nelson' Class and 'S15' Class 4-6-0s, 'Q' Class, 'Z' Class, 'L1' Class and 'D1' Class rebuilds.

The pre-Grouping companies' engines are also featured in the collection and their ranks include; L.&S.W.R. Drummond 'M7' Class 0-4-4Ts, 'T9' Class 4-4-0s and '700' Class 0-6-0. Also making an appearance are; Adams' '415' Class 4-4-2T, 'O2' Class 0-4-4T and 'B4' 0-4-0T, as well as two Beattie '0298' 2-4-0WT locomotives. The S.E.&C.R. Wainwright 'H', 'P', 'D', 'C' and 'L' Classes have been seen by Bill as he rambled over the Southern Region's territory. Completing the selection are Billinton's 'K' 2-6-0s, 'E4' and 'E6' 0-6-2Ts, Stroudley's 'E' or 'E1' 0-6-0s and 'A1' or 'Terrier' Class 0-6-0Ts, all produced for the L.B.&S.C.R.

These classes were photographed at numerous locations across the region. From Greater London in the north, at sheds and stations including Bricklayers Arms, Feltham and Victoria, to Brighton, Southampton and Bournemouth on the south coast. Dover and Folkestone in the south east were visited as well as Exeter, Yeovil and Wadebridge in the south west. The Isle of Wight is also included as the area was incorporated into the S.R. upon Grouping and later the Southern Region of B.R. Bill took photographs of a number of the island's servants at St John's Road shed and lineside at Smallbrook Junction.

This book contains a selection of photographs taken on numerous branch lines around the region and these are particularly evocative of the final years of steam under B.R. operation. From a modern perspective they also give an indication why there was such an eagerness on the part of B.R. for their closure. Many of the lines utilised locomotives that had been in service for a number of years and were perhaps coming to the end of their lifespan. Furthermore, the services operated by the engines often consisted of only one or two carriages and these came under increasing competition for passengers as the use of cars grew.

While some readers may think there has been an omission of certain places or locomotive classes they feel are important to the Southern Region, the intention of the author has been to provide a broad view of the area and the steam engines employed in the last years before the diesel takeover. Fortunately, Bill's passionate interest in steam has made this enthralling collection possible.

Acknowledgements:

I am grateful for the assistance received from the following people: Iris Chambers, Peter Jary, Catherine Mather, Hugh Parkin, Bill Reed, Alan Sutton.

Special thanks are due to my son Tristram for his help and encouragement throughout the project.

Information

I have taken reasonable steps to verify the accuracy of the information in this book but it may contain errors or omissions. Any information that may be of assistance to rectify any problems will be gratefully received. Please contact me by email petertuffrey@rocketmail.com or in writing Peter Tuffrey, 8 Wrightson Avenue, Warmsworth, Doncaster, South Yorkshire, DN4 9QL.

The Last Days of Southern Region Steam

Ashford Shed 33039

Bulleid 'Q1' Class 0-6-0 locomotive no. 33039 has been photographed on the south west side of Ashford shed. Constructed at Brighton Works in December 1942, no. 33039 was the penultimate member of the 40-strong class to enter traffic. Originally the engine was identified as C39, however, by the end of British Railways' first year in operation the number had been changed to 33039. The locomotive was allocated to Battersea at this time, but would move on to St Leonards, Hither Green, Tonbridge and Eastleigh before withdrawal in June 1964.

Ashford Shed 31856
Maunsell 'N' Class 2-6-0 no. 31856 is seen on road no. 3 at Ashford shed, minus the valve gear. Assembled at Ashford Works during March 1925, the engine was condemned in July 1964.

Ashford Shed 31401
No. 31401 was constructed to Maunsell's 'N' Class design at Ashford Works, although some time later, in August 1932. The S.R. looked to employ the class to a greater extent around the system. As a result, the 15 locomotives built conformed to a stricter loading gauge.

Ashford Shed 31255
A number of 0-6-0 goods engines were authorised to be built to the design of Locomotive and Carriage Superintendent H.S. Wainwright by the Board of the South Eastern & Chatham Railway at the turn of the 20th Century. Thirty-six 'C' Class engines were erected in 1900, fifteen of these at Ashford Works, and amongst them was no. 31255, which entered traffic in June.

Ashford Shed 33029
Bulleid 'Q1' no. 33029 as seen from inside Ashford shed. The facilities were installed on a site, to the east of the Canterbury line and north of the Folkestone line, in 1931 to replace an earlier structure located adjacent to Ashford Works. Made from concrete, with a northlight roof, the depot had a coal stage and a 65 ft turntable. Steam locomotives were serviced at the site until June 1962.

Opposite Top
Ashford Station 30936
No. 30936 *Cranleigh*, belonging to the 'Schools' Class, waits for the departure time at the head of an express passenger service from Charing Cross station to Dover.

Opposite Below
Ashford Station 31497
No. 31497 is at Ashford station on 3rd June 1960; the locomotive would be withdrawn by October.

Below
Ashford Station 30938
Ashford station was opened by the South Eastern Railway on 1st December 1842 as part of the company's line to Dover. During the 1990s the station was rebuilt to host Eurostar services and since 8th January 1996 has been called Ashford International station. 'Schools' Class 4-4-0 no. 30938 *St. Olave's* is pictured light engine.

Above
Ashford Shed 31785
Maunsell 'L1' 4-4-0 no. 31785 emerged from the North British Locomotive Company, Glasgow, during April 1926 as part of 15 ordered by the Southern Railway to work on express services to Folkestone.

Opposite Top
Ashford Works 3759
'8750' Class 0-6-0PT engine no. 3759 receives attention in rival territory. Constructed at Swindon in December 1937, this Collett-designed locomotive would be in service until December 1965.

Opposite Bottom
Ashford Shed 31307
No. 31307 was one of 11 engines erected to Wainwright's 'H' Class 0-4-4T design in 1906, being completed at Ashford Works in the final month of the year. The town's depot hosted no. 31307 as the locomotive's career drew to a close and ended in August 1961.

Below

Ashford Works 30935

The South Eastern Railway established Ashford Works in 1847, on land to the south east of the line to Folkestone, and construction of locomotives began in the following year. Upon the S.E.R's amalgamation with the London, Chatham & Dover Railway in 1899, the works became the principal facility for the S.E.&C.R. and was upgraded in the ensuing years. However, when the S.R. was formed at Grouping the honour of being the main works for the new company was handed to Eastleigh. The last steam locomotive was built in 1944 and Ashford subsequently concentrated on repairs until 1962 when this function ceased. Maunsell 'Schools' Class 4-4-0 no. 30935 *Sevenoaks* was erected at Eastleigh in May 1935 and condemned in December 1962. From May 1959 to October 1961 no. 30935 operated from Ashford shed and withdrawal occurred at Nine Elms.

Above

Ashford Shed 33028

Bulleid 'Q1' no. 33028 stands on one of the centre roads serving Ashford shed; a total of ten entered the building. To the left of the locomotive the coal wagons feeding the depot's coal stage can be seen. No. 33028 was completed at Ashford Works in August 1942 and initially allocated to Feltham where employment would have been found on freight services to sites in the London area. At Nationalisation, the engine was transferred to Tonbridge for use on goods trains to Hastings, amongst other destinations, and summer passenger services and excursion specials. Apart from a brief sojourn at Gillingham, no. 33028 was a long-term resident at Tonbridge and did not move again until May 1962 for a brief residency at Feltham. Removal from traffic occurred in February 1963 while at Three Bridges depot.

Above

Axminster Station 30582

The London & South Western Railway introduced William Adams' '415' Class in 1882. No. 30582 appeared in September 1885 from Robert Stephenson & Co.

Opposite Above

Ashford Works 31323

Wainwright's 'P' Class were built for light branch line services. A number of steam railmotors had been tested on these trains previously, but they were discarded through being underpowered, necessitating a new class. The eight 'Ps' were not much more capable and a number were transferred to piloting or shunting duties. However, a small number remained on branch duties, one being no. 31323, which was a long-term employee on the branch between Otford and Sevenoaks. The locomotive was moved to Dover when the Otford line was electrified in the late 1920s and remained on the coast until June 1960. No. 31323 was withdrawn during the month and then sold to the Bluebell Railway where the engine is currently at work.

Opposite Below

Axminster Station 30583

Former L.&S.W.R. Adams '415' Class 4-4-2T no. 30583 has been photographed at Axminster station with a service bound for Lyme Regis. The engine was built by Neilson & Co., Glasgow, in March 1885. The locomotive was later sold to the government during the First World War, then in 1919 to the East Kent Light Railway. The S.R. took the locomotive into their stock during the mid-1940s to provide motive power for services on the Lyme Regis branch line. This remained no. 30583's task until withdrawn in July 1961. The locomotive was subsequently bought by the Bluebell Railway and is currently on display while awaiting repair work to the boiler.

Above

Axminster Station 30582

No. 30582 was one of ten '415' or 'Radial Tank' Class 4-4-2T produced by Robert Stephenson & Co. during 1885; the company had previously supplied 18 engines to the L.&S.W.R. in 1883. Neilson & Co. and Dübs & Co., Glasgow, also completed orders for eleven and ten locomotives respectively in the former year, bringing the class total to 71. No. 30582 rests at Axminster Station on 7th August 1960 before being coupled with a train to Lyme Regis.

Opposite

Axminster Station 30584

Another 'radial tank' preparing to take charge of a passenger service to Lyme Regis was no. 30584, which had been constructed by Dübs & Co. in December 1885 and entered service as L.&S.W.R. no. 520. Axminster station was opened by the L.&S.W.R. on 19th July 1860 as part of the company's line from Yeovil to Exeter. At the former location the route connected with the Salisbury & Yeovil Railway, completed in mid-1860, while at Exeter, Queen Street station was built, but a connection with the Bristol & Exeter Railway at St David's station was formed a short time later. The Yeovil to Exeter line missed some places due to a path being taken through difficult terrain and consequently a number of branch lines were later joined to the route. Over 40 years elapsed, however, before the coastal town of Lyme Regis was connected by rail the L.&S.W.R. line.

Below

Axminster Station 30584 and 30582

Two of the three '415' Class locomotives at work on the Lyme Regis branch have been coupled together to haul a passenger service to the town on 1st August 1960. The gradients on the six-mile branch were often quite steep, requiring the train to climb acclivities to reach the only other station at Combpyne and to pass through the village of Uplyme. The return journey was also similarly graded.

Above

Basingstoke Shed 34009

Bill has caught Bulleid 'Light' or 'West Country' Class Pacific no. 34009 *Lyme Regis* in Basingstoke shed's yard on 14th August 1961 with the Royal Train headlamp code. The locomotive is on a road connected to both the engine shed and the station; a platform belonging to the latter is just visible on the right-hand side. To the left is the depot's 70 ft turntable, which was located on the northern perimeter of the site and installed in 1943. This replaced the original 55 ft example that had been provided when the shed was opened by the L.&S.W.R. in 1905. No. 34009 was constructed at Brighton Works in September 1945 and entered traffic as 21C109 under Bulleid's numbering system. The B.R. number was subsequently applied in March 1949 after the engine had been one of nearly half of the class to carry the 'S' prefix introduced immediately after Nationalisation. *Lyme Regis* had been rebuilt in January 1961, being the first of nine to be transformed in the final year of the reconstruction programme, and remained in service until October 1966.

Below

Basingstoke Shed 30909

Also present at Basingstoke shed was 'Schools' Class engine no. 30909 *St. Paul's*. Erection was completed in July 1930 at Eastleigh Works and the locomotive was the last of the first batch of ten engines ordered initially; the price of this order came to nearly £70,000. These locomotives were numbered in the sequence E900-E909 when entering traffic. E904, E907-9 were sent to Eastbourne shed to be employed on the London services. Working from Guildford at the time of this picture, no. 30909 would be condemned at the shed in February 1962.

Above
Bere Alston 30225
L.&S.W.R. Adams 'O2' Class 0-4-4T locomotive is at the head of the Bere Alston station service to Callington. Entering service from the company's Nine Elms Works in November 1892, no. 30225's career lasted until December 1962 when taken out of stock at Eastleigh shed. The engine was allocated to the depot at Nationalisation, but later found a place at Plymouth Friary shed, working there for several years from the mid-1950s.

Opposite Top
Bournemouth Central Station 35018
Bulleid 'Merchant Navy' Class Pacific no. 35018 *British India Line* emerges from below Holdenhurst Road to enter the eastern end of Bournemouth Central station with the 'Bournemouth Belle' passenger service.

Opposite Bottom
Barnstaple Junction Station 30254
L.&S.W.R. Drummond 'M7' Class 0-4-4T engine no. 30254 is presented here at Barnstaple Junction station. The locomotive was a long-term resident of the depot of the same name which was located on the eastern side of the goods shed, seen on the right of this image at the end of the platform canopy.

Below
Bere Alston Station 30225
Bere Alston station was opened by Plymouth, Davenport & South Western Junction Railway on 1st June 1890 as Beer Alston station and was located on the company's route from Lydford to Devonport. However, operations were carried out by the L.&S.W.R. The name change occurred on 18th November 1897.

Opposite Top
Bournemouth Central Station 34028
Arriving at Bournemouth Central station's western end is Bulleid 'West Country' Pacific no. 34028 *Eddystone*. Erected in April 1946, the locomotive was rebuilt 12 years later in August 1958. Bournemouth station has been renamed twice since opening. In the first instance, 1st May 1899, 'East' was swapped for 'Central;' then on 10th July 1967 'Central' was removed and the station has since been identified simply as Bournemouth.

Opposite Bottom
Bournemouth Shed 30865
Maunsell 'Lord Nelson' Class 4-6-0 no. 30865 *Sir John Hawkins* has been captured by Bill between duties at Bournemouth shed during September 1960.

Below
Bournemouth Central Station 30782
Maunsell 'King Arthur' Class 4-6-0 no. 30782 *Sir Brian* was one of thirty class members built by the N.B.L.C. after Grouping for the S.R. Bournemouth Central signal box dates from the late 1920s and can still be seen at the station.

Above

Bournemouth Shed 30782

No. 30782 *Sir Brian* was also photographed in April 1958 at Bournemouth shed. As with no. 30865, the locomotive is on a section of track extending eastwards from the depot's turntable and this, along with the western section of line, was used for disposing of ash accumulated from the firebox. Also of note is the area behind the locomotive which was previously occupied by the first L.&S.W.R. shed, opened in June 1883 and operational until 1921. The engines built by the N.B.L.C. entered service between May and September 1925; *Sir Brian* was one of four sent to work in July. At Nationalisation, Nine Elms depot housed the engine, then in 1951 two moves occurred; in January a four month residency at Eastleigh began, before Bournemouth became no. 30782's new allocation in June. *Sir Brian* was later condemned at the shed in September 1962.

Below
Bournemouth Shed 30108
During 1888 a four-track building was added to the opposite side of Bournemouth shed yard, but this was enlarged after becoming the sole stabling point from 1921. This was performed by increasing the length of three roads to the west. During a general improvement of the site in 1936 the space was covered over. Amongst 'Merchant Navy' and 'Light' Pacifics is Drummond M7 Class 0-4-4-T no. 30108. Nine Elms Works erected the engine in March 1904 as one of five built to order C12. Five other M7 Class locomotives were constructed during the year to order B12. Bournemouth depot retained the services of no. 30108 between June 1956 and the engine's withdrawal in May 1964.

Bournemouth Shed 30863

The depot's lifting apparatus is visible behind 'Lord Nelson' 4-6-0 no. 30863 *Lord Rodney*. The equipment, with a capacity of 50 tons, was installed at the time of the changes on the site. The locomotive was built at Eastleigh in October 1929 and, like no. 30788, was a casualty in February 1962.

Bournemouth Shed 30788

Maunsell 'King Arthur' Class locomotive no. 30788 *Sir Urre of the Mount* stands on Bournemouth shed's lifting road. Arriving on S.R. metals in September 1925 from the N.B.L.C., no. 30788 was operational until February 1962. During the B.R. era *Sir Urre of the Mount* was predominantly allocated to Eastleigh and is displaying the '71A' shed code in this instance.

Bournemouth Shed 35019

No. 35019 *French Line C.G.T.*, of the 'Merchant Navy' Class, receives attention on the ash road. The engine was rebuilt in May 1959 and would have been equipped with a new ashpan at the time. This was divided into three parts, as had been the case originally, but now featured damper doors.

Opposite Above
Bournemouth Shed 34102
Twenty new 'Light' Pacifics were requested by B.R. in March 1949 under order no. 3486. No. 34102 *Lapford* was completed at Brighton Works as part of this batch in March 1951. Eighteen of these engines belonged to the 'West Country' portion of the Class. *Lapford* has the distinction of being one of the last un-rebuilt 'Light' Pacifics to be withdrawn during July 1967.

Opposite Below
Brighton Shed 30055
Drummond 'M7' Class engine no. 30055 is seen at Brighton shed. The locomotive was built at Nine Elms in December 1905. During the time spent in traffic for B.R., no. 30055 was housed at Brighton from April 1956 to May 1959. Several transfers transpired before the locomotive was taken out of service in September 1963.

Below
Brighton Shed 30902
Under preparation at Brighton shed on 2nd March 1960 was 'Schools' 4-4-0 no. 30902 *Wellington* and the locomotive is seen here on an ash road which ran along the western side of the shed building. Entering service for the S.R. in April 1930, no. 30902 was at work until December 1962 when condemned to be scrapped by B.R. with the 17 other 'Schools' Class members still operational.

Above

Brighton Shed 30839

The L.B.&S.C.R. installed a substantial building and facilities for locomotives at Brighton during 1861, which replaced two servicing points opened by the London & Brighton Railway in 1840 and 1841. The new engine shed contained 16 tracks and was located immediately to the north of Brighton station between the lines to London and Portsmouth. Also provided at this time was a turntable, coal stage and the water tank featured in both of these pictures. Before the Second World War the S.R. embarked upon a refurbishment project at Brighton and the shed building's original multi-pitched roof was replaced with a northlight type roof, then covering only ten roads. This change to the top of the structure necessitated replacing the arched entrances to the shed, which were of the style seen over the windows of the water tank, to plain openings as is discernible on the left of this photograph. Maunsell 'S15' Class 4-6-0 no. 30839 is seen on the eastern side of the shed yard in the early 1960s.

Opposite

Brighton Shed 32340

London, Brighton & South Coast Railway Locomotive Superintendent L.B. Billinton produced a new design for a 2-6-0 or 'Mogul' locomotive in 1913. This was needed to meet the increasing demands of both freight and passenger services on the company's main line between London and Brighton. The 'K' Class design was somewhat a novelty for the L.B.&S.C.R. as the wheel arrangement, use of Belpaire firebox and Weir feedwater heater were new to the railway. Two were constructed initially before a further three were built with some modifications after experience in traffic. No. 32340 was one of the latter and Brighton Works turned the locomotive out during June 1914. The majority of the engine's B.R. career was spent working from Brighton and withdrawal happened at the shed in December 1962.

Brighton Shed 32341
Another 'K' Class 2-6-0 present during Bill's visit was no. 32341, which was constructed at Brighton in November 1914. The locomotive was one of several belonging to the class to be present at the shed for Nationalisation and withdrawal from service by B.R. The date in this instance was December 1962.

Brighton Shed 30538
Norwood Junction-allocated 'Q' Class no. 30583 would transfer to Brighton in March 1961 after several years at the former. The engine's time on the south coast would then last until June 1962.

Brighton Shed 31276
Wainwright 'H' Class locomotive no. 31276's final 18 months were spent working from Brighton depot, having arriving in May 1959 and being condemned in January 1961.

Brighton Shed 32469
R.J. Billinton 'E4' Class 0-6-2T no. 32469 was built at Brighton Works during June 1898 and was in traffic until October 1961.

Below
Brockenhurst Station 30107
Both engine no. 30107 and crew member take a break at Brockenhurst station before working the passenger service from there to Bournemouth West station via Ringwood. The former was opened on 1st June 1847 by the Southampton & Dorchester Railway, which later became part of the L.&S.W.R. Drummond 'M7' Class 0-4-4T locomotive no. 30107 was constructed at Nine Elms Works in April 1905. The engine was noted at Bournemouth shed for Nationalisation and spent the 1950s and early 1960s working from the depot. Withdrawal occurred at the shed in May 1964.

Above

Brighton Shed 30901

'Schools' Class no. 30901 *Winchester* was erected at Eastleigh Works in March 1930 as the second engine from the first order, no. E378. The locomotive entered service as no. E901 as an 'E' prefix was being used at the time to denote that Eastleigh was the designated repair shop for *Winchester*. However, this practice was later discontinued and the 'E' was removed from no. 901 in January 1932. At the time of this photograph *Winchester* had been a recent recipient of B.R. Brunswick green livery, which occurred in June 1960, after spending the last 17 years in S.R. wartime black and B.R. mixed traffic black liveries. A departure from 'official' livery concerns the nameplate as the background should have been black. However, from the end of the 1950s red was applied in a number of instances, returning to S.R. practice for the nameplates of the class. *Winchester* was allocated to Brighton from June 1958 until condemned in December 1962.

Below
Brockenhurst Station 34057
Bulleid 'Battle of Britain' Class Pacific no. 34057 *Biggin Hill* is pictured at Brockenhurst station with a service to Portsmouth and Brighton. The latter town's works built the engine in March 1947 as part of batch no. 3213, which requested a total of 25 new Pacifics. These were originally to conform with the earlier 'Light Pacifics' through being named after towns in the West Country served by the S.R. However, as the 25 engines were to find homes in Hampshire, Surrey and Kent, the decision was taken to find new names for the locomotives. Those eventually chosen honoured the people, squadrons or bases involved with the Battle of Britain. R.A.F. Biggin Hill was one of the main airfields for fighter aircraft taking part in the campaign. No. 34057 was condemned in May 1967.

Above

Brockenhurst Station 30541

S.R. Maunsell 'Q' Class 0-6-0 no. 30541 was erected at Eastleigh Works in January 1939 and initially allocated to Guildford. By Nationalisation Three Bridges depot had taken charge of the engine and then, during September 1953, Bournemouth received the locomotive. No. 30541 has the latter's '71B' shed code in this photograph of the engine at Brockenhurst with a service to the station and Lymington. Moving on to Basingstoke in January 1963, Guildford would be the final transfer in March before B.R. condemned the locomotive for scrap in November 1964. After several years in Woodham Brothers' Barry scrapyard no. 30541 was purchased and restored to working order. The engine is currently owned by the Maunsell Preservation Group and is undergoing overhaul at the Bluebell Railway.

Below

Chard Junction Station 30841

Chard Junction station is the location of this picture of Urie 'S15' Class 4-6-0 no. 30841, which is at the head of a passenger service from Exeter Central station to Yeovil Town station. Chard Junction station was opened as Chard Road on 19th July 1860 and was a stop on the Yeovil - Exeter line. The station was renamed Chard Junction in 1872 and remained open to passengers until 7th March 1966. No. 30841 was constructed at Eastleigh Works during July 1936 and was removed from stock in January 1964. Like no. 30541, no. 30841 was later saved from Barry scrapyard and returned to working order in 1978. After working on the North Yorkshire Moors Railway for several years subsequently, the locomotive was withdrawn for overhaul in the mid-1990s. But, this did not take place and a number of parts were taken for use on classmate no. 30825.

Above
Combpyne Station 30582
No. 30582 rounds the curve taking the Lyme Regis branch line into Combpyne station on 7th August 1960. The engine is at the head of a train from Axminster to the coast. Combpyne station possessed an island platform, which afforded the only place for passing on the line, and stationmaster's house with booking office attached. The three surviving Adams '415' Class locomotives worked the branch until mid-1961 when replaced by Ivatt Class 2 2-6-2T locomotives, which in turn were superseded in November 1963 by diesel railcars. However, this change could not save the line and closure occurred on 29th November 1965.

Above
Dover Shed 30938
'Schools' Class engine no. 30938 *St. Olave's* is seen between tasks at Dover shed. The S.R. built the facilities, which were located to the west of the former site of Dover Town station and to the south of the line to Folkestone, in 1928. The shed, noticeable just to the left of the engine, had five tracks and was made from concrete. B.R. closed the depot to all traffic in June 1961 and the site was cleared, remaining unused.

Opposite Above
Corfe Castle Station 30057
At Corfe Castle station with a service from Swanage is Drummond 'M7' Class locomotive no. 30057. The former closed on 3rd January 1972, but later re-opened as part of the Swanage Railway. The station has recently been modified and this view would now contain a footbridge at the far end of the platform. This was taken from Merton Park station near Wimbledon.

Opposite Below
Dover Shed 31818
Maunsell 'N' Class 2-6-0 no. 31818 was built at Ashford Works in March 1922, having been ordered in 1919. The delay was due to the large amount of rolling stock that was waiting to be overhauled by the works after the end of the First World War. The locomotive is fitted with a '74C' shed plate which represented Dover depot and also happens to be the location for this photograph taken in the late 1950s to early 1960s. No. 31818 would move on to Tonbridge in January 1961 after spending just over ten years at Dover. September 1963 saw the engine leave traffic from Exmouth Junction.

Below

Dunton Green Station 31520

Wainwright 'H' Class 0-4-4T no. 31520 awaits the departure time of a Dunton Green station service to Westerham. The locomotive was built at Ashford Works during June 1909 with Westinghouse bakes and a coal bunker capable of holding 1½ tons of fuel. The last 24 'H' Class engines had this coal capacity, but the first ten engines constructed could carry 2½ tons, while the remaining class members, of the 66 in total, could carry a nominal 2¼ tons. A number of the class were later modified to use 'push and pull' apparatus and no. 31520 was a recipient in June 1949. The locomotive is displaying a '74A' shedcode, signifying an Ashford residency which lasted from May 1958 to May 1959. However, the shedcode was discontinued from October 1958 and a '73F' code would adorn allocated engines from that date.

Above

Dunton Green Station 31533

Another 'H' Class locomotive being used on a Westerham service was no. 31533. Dunton Green station was opened on 2nd March 1868 by the S.E.R. as part of their Tonbridge 'cut-off' line, which greatly reduced the length of the company's main line. The main station building was on the 'up' side, while the 'down' platform had a canopy shelter; both structures being in a similar style to the branch platform shelter seen in this photograph. The signal box seen in the distance was located at the north end of the 'up' platform and dated from the opening of the Westerham branch line.

Above

Eastleigh Shed 4626

G.W.R. Collett '8750' Class 0-6-0PT locomotive no. 4626 appears to have been a recent visitor to Eastleigh Works and is awaiting a return to work, being placed near to the coal stack at Eastleigh shed. No. 4626 was built at Swindon Works during September 1942 as part of lot no. 330, which authorised 50 locomotives. The engine was subsequently employed on 'home' territory until March 1959 when drafted in to help on the lines around Dover. A number of Western Region 0-6-0PT undertook similar duties, but no. 4626 was relieved of this obligation in October 1961 as a transfer to Salisbury took place. Withdrawal from the latter depot occurred during March 1964. Of particular interest in this photograph is the shed code applied to the smokebox door. Under B.R., Dover depot was '74C' from 1950 to 1958, then becoming '73H' until closure in 1961. The former is still in use in this instance.

Opposite

Eastleigh 30378

Running northwards past Eastleigh shed is Drummond 'M7' Class engine no. 30378. Built at Nine Elms Works in May 1903, the locomotive was the last of order H11, for five 'M7s', to enter traffic. Five other class members appeared in 1903 and these marked the start of the use of longer frames for the design; the engines were distinguishable through a greater distance between the smokebox and bufferbeam. No. 30378 left traffic in December 1962.

Eastleigh Shed 34024
'West Country' Pacific no. 34024 *Tamar Valley* has been pictured on 4th March 1961 -
a matter of days after emerging from Eastleigh Works in this new guise.

East Grinstead 31308
Wainwright 'H' Class 0-4-4-T locomotive no. 31308 arrives at East Grinstead station
with a service from Three Bridges station.

Eastleigh Shed 30073
S.R. 'U.S.A.' Class 0-6-0T no. 30073 was one of two class members to have S.R. Malachite green livery, with yellow and black lining, applied while in regular service for B.R. The date of this treatment was November 1963.

Eastleigh Shed 30501
Urie 'S15' Class 4-6-0 no. 30501 was in traffic from June 1920 until June 1963. The locomotive spent the B.R. period working from Feltham depot.

Above

Eastleigh Shed 32506

Bill has encountered Billinton 'E4' Class no. 32506 three months before the end of the 0-6-2T locomotive's career, taking this picture at Eastleigh shed, on the extreme southern end of the eastern coal stage road, during March 1961. The engine was erected at Brighton Works in October 1900, as L.B.&S.C.R. no. 506 *Catherington*, and was later requisitioned for use by the Railway Operating Division, Royal Engineers, seeing service in France between 1917 and 1919. For B.R., the engine undertook duties at Norwood Junction, Brighton, Salisbury, Guildford and Nine Elms before arriving at Eastleigh for the final allocation in January 1961.

Below

Eastleigh Shed 32678

Also photographed during March 1961 was William Stroudley's 'A1' or 'Terrier' Class 0-6-0T locomotive no. 32678. However, unlike no. 32506, this veteran engine would be employed for a further two-and-a-half years before being condemned. No. 32678's career had begun in July 1880 when the engine left Brighton Works (the last member of the class to enter traffic) to take up a position working in London on the suburban trains. Only a decade was spent on these services before the locomotive was transferred south to Portsmouth to handle local branch line passenger services. Also during this period, no. 32678 was one of 17 A1s rebuilt by L.B.&S.C.R. Locomotive, Carriage and Wagon Superintendent D.E. Marsh with a new boiler, being reclassified 'A1X'. The engine was withdrawn in December 1936 after seven years on the Isle of Wight, but was reinstated and later spent a prolonged period working under loan on the Kent & East Sussex Railway. After being taken out of traffic by B.R. in October 1963, no. 32678 was bought by Butlins and after several other owners, returned to the K.&E.S.R. Then, a restoration took place and the locomotive was steamed again in May 1999, now being owned by The Terrier Trust.

Opposite Top
Eastleigh Shed 30532
Maunsell 'Q' Class no. 30532 was constructed at Eastleigh Works in June 1938. A short time later, in March 1941, the locomotive was one of the first class members to receive a cab-side number and 'Southern' lettering on the tender in Bulleid's 'Sunshine' style.

Opposite Bottom
Eastleigh Shed 30096
Built for the L.&S.W.R. to Adams' 'B4' Class 0-4-0T design for dock shunting work, no. 30096's career spanned 70 years before withdrawal by B.R. in October 1963. A further nine years were spent working for Corralls, Southampton, before being acquired by the Bulleid Preservation Society in 1972. No. 30096 was operational on the Bluebell Railway between 1986 and 2006 and is currently on display awaiting a return to steam.

Below
Eastleigh Shed 32646
'A1X' Class 0-6-0T no. 32646 was also present at Eastleigh during March 1961. Like classmate no. 32678, the locomotive has entered preservation and is working on the Isle of Wight Steam Railway at present.

Eastleigh Shed 30274
Adams 'G6' 0-6-0T locomotive no. 30274 is seen out of traffic at Eastleigh shed with Standard Class 4 2-6-0 no. 76058.

Eastleigh Shed 30865
'Lord Nelson' Class locomotive no. 30865 *Sir John Hawkins* was allocated to Eastleigh from November 1959 until withdrawal in May 1961. This latter was only two months away when the picture was taken.

Eastleigh Shed 30028
Resting on the eastern side of Eastleigh shed is Drummond 'M7' Class locomotive no. 30028, which was based at the depot from June 1956 until condemned in September 1962.

Eastleigh Shed 34043
Bulleid 'West Country' Pacific no. 34043 *Coombe Martin* was erected at Brighton Works in October 1946 and was employed by B.R. until June 1963.

Below
Eastleigh Shed 34101

'West Country' Class no. 34101 *Hartland* was one of twenty 'Light Pacifics' ordered from Brighton Works as part of order no. 3486. However, as the works were in the midst of producing Bulleid's 'Leader' Class locomotives, the task of constructing six engines of the batch was transferred to Eastleigh Works. No. 34101 was one and entered traffic in February 1950, featuring a drop grate instead of the standard rocking grate. *Hartland* only spent a little over ten years in original condition before being rebuilt in September 1960, returning to work at Stewarts Lane depot, Battersea, where the locomotive had been allocated from new. A reallocation occurred every year between 1961 and 1964, the final move taking no. 34101 to Eastleigh and withdrawal would occur at the shed in July 1966. *Hartland* had one of the lowest mileages from being rebuilt to the latter date with approx. 330,100 miles accumulated in traffic.

Above
Eastleigh Shed 30515
A concentration of engine sheds occurred around Eastleigh, Bishopstoke station and the L.&S.W.R. works from the 1840s as three buildings were completed. In addition, a major facility, known as Northam depot, was provided next to Southampton Terminus station. However, at the turn of the century the decision was made to close all of the above sheds. Construction of a new depot to the south of the works and Gosport line and east of the line into Southampton was authorised and finished during 1903. The new building contained 15 tracks and, originally, a slated roof covered them. The coal stage was of the ramp type and the turntable was 55 ft diameter. Repair facilities were also provided on the west side of the building. This view of Urie 'S15' Class locomotive no. 30515 was taken looking northwards from the coal stage ramp.

Previous Page
Eastleigh Shed 30476
Urie 'H15' Class 4-6-0 no. 30476 was constructed at Eastleigh Works in April 1924 and in service until December 1961, being withdrawn from Eastleigh shed. The B.R. emblem on the tender is facing the wrong way.

Above
Eastleigh Shed 30802
Maunsell 'King Arthur' Class 4-6-0 no. 30802 *Sir Durnore* is pictured outside Eastleigh shed on 5th September 1960.

Opposite Top
Eastleigh Shed 32662
'A1X' no. 32662 has also been preserved and at the present time is based at Bressingham, although not in steam. The locomotive was built at Brighton Works during October 1875, received the improved boiler in December 1912 and left B.R. service in November 1963. This was while at Eastleigh, where the engine had spent the preceding six months.

Opposite Bottom
Eastleigh Shed 31916
S.R. 'W' Class 2-6-4T no. 31916 has been photographed on Eastleigh shed's western side, which featured the repair shop and sand kiln, seen behind the engine to the right. Eastleigh-allocated in May 1961, no. 31916 was sent for scrap in July 1963.

Exeter St David's Station 34060

Two generations of enthusiasts admire Bulleid's 'Battle of Britain' Pacific no. 34060 *25 Squadron* on 30th August 1960. The locomotive would only have this appearance for a short period, however, as by November 1960 no. 34060 had been rebuilt. G.W.R. Collett 'Grange' Class 4-6-0 no. 6830 *Buckenhill Grange* can be seen a short distance down platform five at Exeter St David's station.

Eastleigh Shed 31735

S.E.&C.R. Wainwright 'D' Class 4-4-0 no. 31735 was constructed by Sharp, Stewart & Co., but was exhibited in Glasgow before entering service November 1901. The design was introduced to work the heaviest trains on the S.E.&C.R. lines. However, by the early 1920s the loadings had increased past the capabilities of the locomotives. Maunsell thus modified the design to make the engines more powerful and a number were rebuilt. No. 31735 was sent to Beyer, Peacock & Co. and returned transformed in August 1921.

Eastleigh Shed 30117

Drummond's 'T9' Class 4-4-0 design was the answer to the heavier trains operating on the L.&S.W.R's routes. No. 30117 was built at Nine Elms Works during July 1899 and was in service until July 1961.

Above

Exeter St David's Station 34060

No. 34060 *25 Squadron* as viewed from a different angle at Exeter St David's station. The engine's career began during April 1947 as 21C160, but by October 1948 *25 Squadron* had acquired the B.R. number. Also during this period, the locomotive received a v-shaped cab front to increase forward visibility, both during the day and night. Another modification carried out on the class from 1952 involves the safety valves, which are liberating steam into the atmosphere in this photograph. The three Ross 'pop' safety valves employed were originally sited on the front barrel section of the boiler. However, under vigorous braking, water in the boiler would surge forward and be released via the safety valves, often in unsuitable locations, such as stations. Thus, the valves were moved rearwards behind the steam dome. No. 34060 was withdrawn in July 1967.

Below
Exeter St David's Station 30956
S.R. Maunsell 'Z' Class 0-8-0T no. 30956 was also at work at Exeter St David's station on 30th August 1960. The engine had been built at Brighton Works during March 1929 as part of the only batch to be erected, which consisted of eight locomotives. The work was originally to be completed at Ashford, but because the facilities were at capacity the order was transferred to the aforementioned shops, which, incidentally, estimated the cost per engine to be 250£ more than Brighton actually produced them for. The total cost for the eight locomotives was 49,160£. At the time of this picture no. 30956 was 'on the books' at Exmouth Junction depot and had been there since April 1956; withdrawal would occur at the shed in December 1962.

Opposite Top
Exeter St David's Station 34108
No. 34108 *Wincanton* enters the south end of Exeter St David's station with a passenger service from the east; the lines in the right of the picture head to the south west of England. The locomotive was erected in April 1950 and rebuilt in May 1961, being one of the last two class members to be so treated.

Opposite Bottom
Exeter St David's Station 34029
'West Country' no. 34029 *Lundy* has been photographed during the summer of 1958. The locomotive has B.R. standard livery with lining extending across both locomotive and tender, in addition to a black splasher band running above the wheels. However, this would soon be altered. During the rebuilding process, which took place in December 1958, the tender's side plates would be reduced in height and the livery lining altered to follow the contours of the cab and tender.

Below
Exeter St David's Station 34033
'West Country' Pacific no. 34033 *Chard* was one of two class members to be fitted with spark arresters after Nationalisation. The locomotive was given a type used by the London Midland Region in January 1949, while no. 34034 *Honiton* received a pattern designed at Brighton. However, both arrangements were detrimental to the operation of the locomotives and saw quick removal; the date for no. 34033 was June 1949.

Above

Exmouth Junction Shed 30719

Exmouth Junction shed was located a distance to the east of both Exeter St David's and Queen Street stations, close to the junction that provided the name for the depot, where the L.&S.W.R. diverged southwards to Exmouth. The aforementioned company erected the depot on the north side of the line to Exeter towards the end of 1887. The structure, which covered 11 tracks, was formed from a metal frame being covered in iron sheeting; this was also the material used for the roof which had four gables. Prior to Grouping the L.&S.W.R. authorised the reconstruction of the depot, but this was not completed until 1927. The new shed was made from the more durable concrete and had an extra road under the northlight roof. A mechanical coaling plant and 65 ft turntable brought the facilities further up to date. No. 30719, of the 'T9' Class and pictured at the same time as no. 30712, was erected by Dübs & Co. in September 1899 and in traffic until March 1961. The locomotive's final allocation was to Exmouth Junction, arriving in May 1959.

Opposite

Exmouth Junction Shed 30712

Seen against the southern wall of Exmouth Junction shed during April 1958 is Drummond 'T9' Class 4-4-0 no. 30712. The locomotive was one of thirty examples of the class commissioned from Dübs & Co., Glasgow, and constructed during 1899; as L.&S.W.R. no. 712, the engine entered service in June of that year. The livery for the class at this time would have been Drummond passenger green with lining in black and white. No. 30712 is photographed with B.R. mixed traffic black with red and white lining applied, as was the case with the remainder of the class after Nationalisation. The locomotive arrived at Exmouth Junction in January 1951 and was condemned at the shed during November 1958.

Exmouth Junction Shed 34030

'West Country' Pacific no. 34030 *Watersmeet* stands in the shed yard at Exmouth Junction during April 1958. The locomotive was completed in May 1946 and remained unaltered when withdrawn during September 1964. Thirty 'Light' Pacifics were condemned during the year, while twelve left traffic during the month. No. 34033 *Chard* is the 'West Country' partially in view on the left.

Exmouth Junction Shed 30689
Drummond '700' Class 0-6-0 no. 30689 was built by Dübs & Co. in March 1897. The locomotive was subsequently removed from stock at Exmouth Junction in November 1962. However, the engine had evidently been called back into service for snow plough duties when pictured on 24th February 1963.

Exmouth Junction Shed 30451
Maunsell 'King Arthur' 4-6-0 no. 30451 *Sir Lamorak* prepares to return home to Salisbury during April 1958. The engine was based there from 1950 until June 1962.

Above

Exmouth Junction Shed 30024

Dugald Drummond arrived at the L.&S.W.R. during 1895, taking the position of Locomotive Engineer, later retitled Chief Mechanical Engineer. He had previously enjoyed similar positions with the North British Railway and Caledonian Railway in Scotland. Drummond had produced two classes to the 0-4-4T wheel arrangement for both companies, N.B.R. Class 'P' and C.R. '171' Class, and these, in addition to Adams' 'T1' Class, provided inspiration for his 'M7' Class. No. 30024 was built to the design at Nine Elms Works in January 1899 and continued to be in traffic until condemned, while at Bournemouth, in March 1963. The locomotive is seen at Exmouth Junction shed during April 1958.

Opposite

Exmouth Junction Shed 34061

As the Bulleid Pacifics' inside motion was housed in an oil bath, wear around the seals inevitably caused the contents to leak and cover the lagging around the boiler. The wheels could also find themselves coated with the substance causing the class further problems with wheel-slipping. The build up of oil on the boiler cladding, however, could result in serious fires breaking out when introduced to a form of ignition, which was readily available from the firebox, chimney and even the brake shoes. Suspicions fell heavily on the former after Nationalisation and several class members were experimentally fitted in February 1949 with a water spray system to cool the contents of the ashpan before any stray lubricant could be ignited. No. 34061 *73 Squadron*, which is seen here being serviced at Exmouth Junction's ash pits during April 1958, was one such locomotive fitted, while the others were nos 34001, 34005 and 34062. This arrangement did not entirely cure the need to call the nearest fire brigade and was later removed, but an earlier attempt to stop the occurrences of fire was adopted class-wide. Fire retardant sheets made from steel were fitted around the firebox and boiler; no. 34042 *Dorchester* was the first recipient in June 1948.

Opposite

Exmouth Station 30024

Paired with Ivatt Class '2' 2-6-2T no. 41306 at Exmouth station is Drummond 'M7' Class locomotive no. 30024. The station was opened by the L.&S.W.R. on 1st May 1861 as the terminus for a branch from the Yeovil to Exeter line. Subsequently, Exmouth station moved a short distance away from the original position when rebuilding work to reduce the number of platforms took place in the early 1970s. The terminus was again ready for passengers on 2nd May 1976. No. 41306 was one of 130 locomotives constructed by both the L.M.S. and B.R. to Ivatt's design. The engine left Crewe Works in April 1952, beginning work at Faversham and later being posted at Exmouth Junction. No. 41306 was at the depot from June 1955 until condemned to be scrapped in December 1963.

Opposite

Exmouth Junction Shed 34011

While 'West Country' Pacific no. 34011 *Tavistock* was perhaps only too happy to pose for Bill's camera, the footplateman changing the headcode shows what he thinks of having his picture taken. The locomotive was one of three 'Light' Pacifics erected at Brighton during October 1945. Shortly after being released into traffic, *Tavistock* had the honour of being displayed at Ashford for the town's Thanksgiving Week celebrations. The locomotive also had the distinction of being inspected by the Institution of Mechanical Engineers while under general repair in mid-1947 at Brighton Works. Particular interest was shown towards the inside motion arrangement and the group was said to be particularly moved by the cleanliness of the components. No. 34011 is distinguished further through being one of a few class members to have an Apple green livery applied after Nationalisation as B.R. sought standard colour schemes for locomotives. *Tavistock* had the livery between May 1948 and September 1950. No. 34011 had a number of associations with Exmouth Junction depot and would be withdrawn there in November 1963.

Above

Folkestone Junction Sidings 4610

As at Dover, a number of Western Region 0-6-0PT locomotives were brought in to Folkestone by the S.R. to assist on some duties, such as the trains on the Folkestone Harbour branch line, which was especially steep. Two 0-6-0PT engines have been caught by Bill waiting for the next turn in Folkestone Junction sidings. These were located to the south of the station and on the west side of the line to Folkestone Harbour. No. 4610 is seen in the foreground while the engine in the background cannot be identified. The former was one of five '8750' Class locomotives to be constructed at Swindon Works during February 1942. After leaving Barry shed in March 1959, no. 4610 had spells at Dover, Feltham, Weymouth and Exmouth Junction before leaving service in October 1964.

Opposite

Folkestone Junction Shed 30900

At the entry point to Folkestone Junction shed is the first 'Schools' Class locomotive, no. 30900 *Eton*. Located on land just to the north of Folkestone Junction station's eastern side, the depot dated from 1900 and would be in use until mid-1961. No. 30900 entered service from Eastleigh Works in March 1930 without smoke deflectors, as did the following nine engines. Solving the problem of smoke drifting around the cab and obscuring the view of the footplatemen was attempted by the majority of the 'big four' railway companies in the late 1920s and early 1930s. The 'Schools' Class were to have them, but delays in arriving at the right arrangement for the engines caused their omission from the first ten. The National Physical Laboratory, where a number of other smoke deflector designs were developed, held test with a scale model concluded that the plates should be straight and project forward towards the bufferbeam to direct more air towards the exhaust. The first ten 'Schools' acquired this type between mid-1931 and the end of 1932.

Below
Halwill Station 31842
Maunsell 'N' Class 2-6-0 no. 31842 heads eastwards through Halwill station with a mixed freight service. No. 31842 was one of fifty 'N' Class locomotives to have the majority of their parts, except the boiler which was fabricated by the N.B.L.C., to be produced by Woolwich Arsenal after the factory stopped making armaments upon the end of the First World War. Ashford Works brought the components together and no. 31842, as no. A842, was sent into traffic during August 1924. The locomotive has subsequently been modified through the addition of smoke deflectors and outside steam pipes. This latter alteration occurred in December 1957 and also resulted in the replacement of the main frames. No. 31842 was condemned in September 1965 while at Guildford shed.

Above

Folkestone Junction Station 34073

Folkestone Junction station was first opened on a temporary basis from 28th June 1843 by the S.E.R., but this was soon superseded by the permanent stop on 18th December 1843. At first the station was referred to as Folkestone. However, names subsequently applied, for varying periods, included; Folkestone Old, Folkestone Junction and Folkestone Junction Shorncliffe. From 10th September 1962 the station was renamed Folkestone East and this remained in use until closure occurred on 6th September 1965; the site was later cleared. Bulleid 'Battle of Britain' Pacific no. 34073 *249 Squadron* is seen at the head of an eastbound train on 4th May 1960.

Above
Halwill Station 30715
The Devon & Cornwall Railway opened a route between Meldon Junction, on the line from Exeter to Plymouth near Okehampton, and Holsworthy on 20th January 1879. One of the stations on the route was Halwill, which opened as Halwill & Beaworthy, and services were operated from the outset by the L.&S.W.R. When the North Cornwall Railway installed a line to Launceston, and later Wadebridge and Padstow, from Halwill, the station was renamed Halwill Junction from the opening of the route on 21st July 1886. A further change occurred in 1922 after the commencement of services on the Torrington branch as the station became Halwill for Beaworthy. Drummond 'T9' Class 4-4-0 no. 30715 pauses at Halwill on 31st August 1960 with a mixed passenger and freight train.

Below
Halwill Station 31853
Captured from the 'down' platform at Halwill, looking south, is Maunsell 'N' Class locomotive no. 31853. The main building was on this side of the station, while the 'up' platform featured the signal box amongst several other small structures. The signal box was upgraded after the opening of the Launceston line, and again after the Torrington connection, with this latter giving rise to the box's unusual appearance. Also on the 'down' side was a goods yard with turntable. Two extensions of this area were later carried out by the L.&S.W.R. and S.R. during World War Two. Freight services ceased on 7th September 1964 and by 3rd October 1966 Halwill had closed to passengers. Houses have subsequently been erected on the station site and part of the trackbed is a cycle path and nature reserve.

Opposite Top
Hawkhurst Station 31519
Wainwright 'H' Class 0-4-4T no. 31519 has completed a Paddock Wood to Hawkhurst station passenger service. Displaying an Ashford shed code, the engine resided at the depot between May 1958 and May 1959.

Opposite Bottom
Hawkhurst Station 31520
Reaching the end of the line with the same service was classmate no. 31520. After leaving Ashford shed, the locomotive spent just over a year at Tonbridge before withdrawal occurred in August 1960.

Below
Havant Station 32661
Stroudley 'A1' Class 0-6-0T no. 32261 is pictured at Havant station on 16th September 1960. The locomotive was constructed at Brighton in October 1875 and withdrawn in April 1963, being the last class member to be scrapped at the hands of B.R.

Above

Hawkhurst Station 31500

The Cranbrook & Paddock Wood Railway initiated the proposals to construct a line between the two places during the 1870s. However, financial difficulties caused the scheme to be re-evaluated and a second act was obtained in the 1880s, but the route now extended to Hawkhurst. The branch line left the S.E.R's London to Folkestone line at Paddock Wood and the first six miles to Hope Mill for Goudhurst & Lamberhurst were ready for traffic on 1st October 1892. Hawkhurst station saw services begin on 4th September 1893. No. 31500 was erected at Ashford Works in November 1905 and in service until June 1961; the line also closed during the month. The station and water tank were later demolished, while the signal box remained standing for a number of years and was subject to a preservation attempt, but this was unfortunately unsuccessful.

Below

Horsted Keynes Station 30055

Drummond 'M7' Class locomotive no. 30055 arrives at Horsted Keynes station with a passenger service from Haywards Heath station. The former opened on 1st August 1882 as part of the Lewes & East Grinstead Railway line between the two towns, which was operated by the L.B.&S.C.R. In the following year the latter company opened a connecting line between Haywards Heath, on the London and Brighton line, and Horsted Keynes; this was later electrified in the mid-1930s. The Lewes to East Grinstead line was closed during 1958 after a fight between local residents and B.R., while the route to Haywards Heath followed on 28th October 1963. Horsted Keynes was taken out of B.R. employment at this time after remaining active for the latter route. The 1958 closure led to the formation of a preservation group and part of the line between Sheffield Park and Horsted Keynes was reopened as the Bluebell Railway during 1962. Subsequently, the railway has extended to East Grinstead and there is a possibility of reconnecting with Haywards Heath.

Below
Isle of Wight Ryde St John's Road Shed W16
L.&S.W.R. Adams 'O2' Class 0-4-4T locomotive no. W16 *Ventnor* is seen on a track between St John's Road shed and station, Ryde, Isle of Wight. The station's signal box is also present on the right and this still controls the traffic at St John's Road. W16 was built at Nine Elms Works in June 1892 as no. 217; from October 1925 to December 1934 the locomotive's number had an 'E' prefix to denote that Eastleigh was responsible for repairing the engine. In 1936 no. 217 was relocated to the Isle of Wight and took the number W16, also being named *Ventnor* after the resort on the island's south coast. Removal from traffic came in January 1967.

Above

Isle of Wight Ryde Pier Head Station W26

The L.&S.W.R. and L.B.&S.C.R. joined forces in the late 1870s to improve landing facilities at the Isle of Wight for their respective ferries from south of England ports. A new pier was built and connected to Ryde St John's Road station by rail. The first section of this link was opened from the latter to Ryde Esplanade station on 5th April 1880 and the final part followed to Pier Head station on 12th July 1880. Adams 'O2' locomotive no. W26 *Whitwell* leaves Pier Head station with a passenger service during the early 1960s.

Above

Isle of Wight Ryde St John's Road Shed W31

A servicing point for locomotives at Ryde St John's Road station was first installed by the Isle of Wight Railway in August 1864. This was made from brick, had two roads and was located on the east side of the station. The building was only in use for ten years then being amalgamated into workshops servicing the I.O.W.R's locomotive and rolling stock. The new shed was made from corrugated iron, but located south of the station and on the west side of the line. This was in use for a good deal longer than the predecessor and closure happened in 1930. Erected using concrete bricks and asbestos, the new two-track structure was built on land to the north. No. W31 *Chale* rests on the east road at the shed on 19th August 1960.

Opposite

Isle of Wight Ryde St John's Road Shed W35

Pictured on the west side of Ryde St John's Road shed, which can be seen in the background, is another of Adams' 'O2' Class engines - no. W35 *Freshwater*. Entering traffic from Nine Elms Works in May 1890 as L.&S.W.R. no. 181, the locomotive was not employed on the Isle of Wight until after Nationalisation. Upon arrival W35 became one of only two class members on the island to be fitted with 'push and pull' train apparatus. Withdrawal occurred in October 1966.

Above

Isle of Wight Ryde St John's Road Shed W18

Having the fire grate cleaned on the ash road at St John's Road is no. W18 *Ningwood*. The ash facilities were located on the west side of the building and the track ran along the eastern side of the depot's ramped coal stage. St John's Road closed at the end of December 1966 as the use of steam by B.R. on the Isle of Wight came to an end. The site was cleared soon afterwards.

Opposite

Isle of Wight Ryde St John's Road Shed W4

Stroudley's 'E' Class were initially intended as goods locomotives, but subsequently their use on passenger traffic grew. This locomotive, L.B.&S.C.R. no. 131 *Gournay* (constructed at Brighton Works in October 1878), moved to the Isle of Wight in June 1933, becoming no. W4 *Wroxhall* in the process. Three other 'E' Class engines, later classified 'E1' under Billinton, had arrived on the island in the preceding year and took the numbers W1-3. *Wroxhall* had been at work from Ryde for just under 30 years when condemned in October 1960. Interestingly, the railings seen here, located on the shed's western perimeter, are still present at the site and now enclose the station's car park.

Below
Isle of Wight Ryde St John's Road Shed W22
'O2' Class no. W22 *Brading* was constructed at Nine Elms Works in June 1892 as part of order no. D4, which specified 20 engines of Adams' design were to be built; the task was completed between December 1891 and November 1892. Originally L.&S.W.R. no. 215, the engine became W22 *Brading* after transfer to the Isle of Wight in 1924. A further alteration carried out after 1932 was an increase to the coal capacity, which was 1 ton 10 cwt when new, to 3 tons 5 cwt; the water capacity remained unaltered at 800 gallons. Also fitted was Westinghouse brake equipment that can be seen here mounted next to the smokebox, with the vacuum reservoir present on top of the water tank. W22 was condemned on 1st January 1967.

Above

Isle of Wight Ryde St John's Road Station W24

The I.O.W.R. opened Ryde St John's Road station on 23rd August 1864 as Ryde station; the remainder of the title was used from 1880. After the end of steam, the station was closed between 1st January 1967 and 20th March 1967 for the electrification of the line. Stock formerly used on the London Underground was introduced at this time, classified 451 and 452, later 485 and 486, and was in use until replaced by more trains previously employed below the capital. No. W24 *Calbourne* is seen with a passenger service just south of the station, with the engine shed visible to the left of the locomotive, in the early 1960s.

Below
Isle of Wight Smallbrook Junction W18
Ryde was connected to Newport by rail at the end of 1875 when the Ryde & Newport opened their line from Smallbrook Junction and the I.O.W.R. line. The R.&N.R. later became part of the Isle of Wight Central Railway when the company formed in the late 1880s. Adams 'O2' Class no. W18 *Ningwood* was constructed at Nine Elms Works during September 1892 as L.&S.W.R. no. 220 and was in service until December 1965; 35 years were spent at work on the Isle of Wight. W18 is travelling in the vicinity of Smallbrook Junction during the early 1960s.

Above
Isle of Wight Smallbrook Junction W26
Another Adams 'O2' locomotive built to order no. D4 at Nine Elms Works was no. 210, which was completed during December 1891. In 1925 the engine was relieved of mainland duties and became W26 *Whitwell* to continue working for the S.R. on the Isle of Wight. All of the engines employed on there took names of places on the island and Whitwell is a village located near the south coast, being also in close proximity to Ventnor. W26 left traffic in May 1966.

Below
Isle of Wight Smallbrook Junction W30
A total of 23 'O2' Class locomotives were sent across the Solent to the Isle of Wight. Two arrived initially in 1923 and this number was steadily added to for the rest of the decade as two more came ashore in 1924, four in 1925 and 1926, one in 1927 followed by no. 226, W32 *Bonchurch*, in 1928. Five more were transferred in the 1930s, two in 1930 and three in 1936, and the final four came in the late 1940s. W30 *Shorwell* began work in 1926 and remained in service until September 1965.

Above
Isle of Wight Smallbrook Junction W36
Heading south, after passing under Smallbrook Lane road bridge, is W36 *Carisbrooke*, which was the other 'O2' class member to operate with 'push and pull' train apparatus. The I.O.W.R. opened the line from Ryde to Shanklin on 23rd August 1864 and this remains part of the island's railway network. The I.O.W.C.R's track from Smallbrook Junction was closed in early 1966, but approx. five miles of rails have since been put back into use for steam services under the Isle of Wight Steam Railway. In 1991 Smallbrook Junction station was opened to allow passengers to switch between the steam railway and the island's main line.

Above

Isle of Wight Ventnor Station W28

The I.O.W.R. line was authorised to run to Ventnor, but because of disputes over the land this part of the line passed over, the opening was delayed until 10th September 1866. Falling just short of celebrating a centenary, the station was closed on 18th April 1966. The site has since been cleared and is presently occupied by an industrial estate, while the tunnel under St Boniface Down has been bricked up, but not filled in. The I.O.W.R. route remains open between Ryde and Shanklin. W28 *Ashey* was operational between July 1890 and January 1967 and was on the Isle of Wight from 1926.

Opposite

Isle of Wight Ventnor Station W14

W14 *Fishbourne* was one of the first ten 'O2' Class locomotives to be constructed at Nine Elms Works, under order no. O2 for ten engines, in 1889, entering traffic during December as L.&S.W.R. no. 178. After Grouping the locomotive carried the 'E' prefix between 1926 and 1932, but it was not until mid-1936 that the 'W' prefix was used in conjunction with the engine's new number. *Fishbourne* is pictured at Ventnor station in the early 1960s. No. W14 would be in service until December 1966; only three locomotives of order no. O2 failed to be in service for the start of the 1960s.

Above

London Bricklayers Arms Shed 32417

The engine sheds at Bricklayers Arms were squeezed into space between the S.E.R's goods depot and the L.,B.&S.C.R's goods facilities. The first shed dated from 1st May 1844 when the S.E.R's station opened, originally to serve passengers. The former was joined by a four-road building in 1847, which is the shed seen behind no. 31293. Another structure with four roads was added to the south west side of the above in 1865. The next addition comprised a six-track shed to the north east and was erected in 1869. During the Second World War this was badly damaged and was not subsequently repaired, being used for storing out of service engines. This is the location of Billinton 'E6' Class 0-6-2T no. 32417, which was pictured by Bill on 11th March 1961. The locomotive would subsequently return to work and be withdrawn from Brighton in December 1962.

Opposite

London Bricklayers Arms Shed 31293

S.E.&C.R. Wainwright 'C' Class 0-6-0 no. 31293 stands outside Bricklayers Arms 'old' shed, London, on 11th March 1961. The locomotive entered traffic from Ashford Works during June 1908 and was sent new to Bricklayers Arms depot, which was located next to Bricklayers Arms goods station at the end of a mile-long branch from New Cross. In addition to the intended goods traffic role, the locomotive was used to take empty carriage stock to both Cannon Street and Charing Cross stations. For this, no. 31293 was equipped for steam heating the trains, as were nos 280, 294 and 297, which also went to the shed for their first allocation. By Nationalisation, no. 31293 had transferred to Stewarts Lane and this was quickly followed by a move to Guildford where employment was found on local goods duties after the withdrawal of older locomotives. Returning to the capital during the 1950s, the engine would be withdrawn from Bricklayers Arms in May 1962.

Above

London Feltham Shed 30032

On the south side of Feltham depot is Drummond 'M7' no. 30032. The shed and facilities were brought into use gradually over the period immediately before and after Grouping. The scheme had been set in motion by the L.&S.W.R. and land was chosen to the east of Feltham station and on the south side of the line to Windsor and Reading. Concrete was used as the building material, while the roof was of the northlight pattern. A repair shop, 65 ft turntable and mechanical coaler with 200 tons capacity were provided. No. 30032 was built at Nine Elms Works in March 1898 and was in service until July 1963. Feltham shed was closed in July 1967 and the site later cleared, now being occupied by a business park.

Opposite

London Bricklayers Arms Shed 30930

Looking north-westwards at the rear of the old engine shed at Bricklayers Arms on 18th May 1962, 'Schools' Class 4-4-0 no. 30930 *Radley* has been captured at the ash pits. Behind the engine is B.R. Standard Class 4 2-6-4T locomotive no. 80094 and the shed's repair shop, which was constructed in the mid-1930s. The shop was capable of heavy repairs through the possession of a wheel drop and overhead crane. No. 30930 was the first of three class members erected in January 1935 as part of the final order to be placed, E496, for ten engines. All of the 'Schools' Class were balanced for 30% of the reciprocating masses, but this was not strictly necessary due to the use of three cylinders. After the arrival of Bulleid in the late 1930s, his technical assistant Harold Holcroft suggested that the balancing should be modified. This was implemented on several class members, *Radley* being one sometime in the late 1930s to early 1940s, and the alteration is visible here; the crescent weights have been replaced with shorter flat-edged weights. No. 30930 is in the midst of a year-long allocation to Redhill depot and withdrawal would take place at the end of this.

Above

London Hither Green Shed 31682

Waiting for the next assignment to begin, outside no. 4 road at Hither Green shed on 6th September 1960, iss Wainwright 'C' Class 0-6-0 no. 31682. Two batches of fifteen 'C' Class locomotives were ordered from contractors when the design was initially authorised. Neilson, Reid & Co., later one of the companies which amalgamated to form the N.B.L.C., completed S.E.&C.R. nos 681-695 in June and July 1901, with no. 31682 emerging in the former month. The total cost for this order was £48,000. Sharp, Stewart & Co. was the other supplier and their engines were sent into traffic between December 1900 and January 1901. The company's cost per locomotive was 30£ cheaper than Neilson, Reid & Co., leading to a total of 47,550£ for the fifteen. No. 31682 was allocated to Hither Green at the time of the photograph and would be condemned at the depot in October 1961.

Opposite

London Feltham Shed 32408

Billinton 'E6' Class 0-6-2T no. 32408 was constructed at Brighton Works in December 1904 as the second member of the class and one of the first eight to be named, carrying the name *Binderton*. The 'E6' Class comprised a total of twelve engines, which were built to shunt freight and head medium distance goods trains. No. 32408 has the distinction of being one of the final three 'E6s' to be withdrawn from service in December 1962; the other two were nos 32417 and 32418. The locomotive is depicted on Feltham shed's southern side, near the ash pits, on 11th March 1961.

Above

London Hither Green 33010

Bulleid 'Q1' Class 0-6-0 locomotive no. 33010 was erected at Brighton Works during September 1942. However, a number of the S.R.'s other workshops had a role in building not only this engine, but the other members of the class as well. Eastleigh Works fabricated the boilers, which were similar in design to those used by the 'Lord Nelson' Class, while Ashford and Lancing Carriage Works completed the tender frames and tank respectively. No. 33010, as no. C10, was allocated new to Guildford and remained at the shed until Nationalisation when a move to Feltham had occurred. The latter housed the locomotive until condemned in January 1964.

Opposite

London Hither Green Shed 31855

The late 1930s saw the water system at Hither Green shed improved through the addition of a 5,000 gallon water softener after the negative effects of the area's hard water had been experienced. The tender of Maunsell 'N' Class 2-6-0 no. 31855 is filled at the depot with an S.R. 'boom' type water column, reminiscent of the kind previously used by the L.B.&S.C.R., during the early 1960s. The locomotive had been erected at Ashford Works, using parts acquired from Woolwich Arsenal, in March 1925 and was paired with the class standard Maunsell straight-sided 3,500 gallon tender with nominal five-ton coal capacity; the total weight of the tender was 39 tons 5 cwt. No. 31855 would leave traffic in September 1964.

Above

London Hither Green Shed 31695

No. 31695 was also built as part of the 15 ordered from Neilson, Reid & Co. and was the last to head to the south of England in July 1900. Hither Green shed was commissioned by the S.R. and ready for traffic in 1933. The shed was situated to the south of Hither Green station on the east side of the Tonbridge 'cut-off' line and the west side of the line to Dartford. Six tracks were contained in the building, which was constructed from concrete and asbestos, and repair facilities, such as a wheel drop, were also accommodated. The turntable was 65 ft diameter, located on the north-eastern perimeter of the site, and the coal stage was ramped and found on the eastern side. No. 31695's 4½-ton capacity tender is replenished during the early 1960s.

Below
London Hither Green Shed 31783
S.R. Maunsell 'L1' Class 4-4-0 no. 31783 was constructed by the
N.B.L.C. in April 1926 and was in traffic until November 1961. During
the time spent in B.R. service the engine had long-standing allocations
to Bricklayers Arms and Nine Elms depots.

Above

London Nine Elms Shed 31768

No. 31768 was one of several engines used by the Locomotive Club of Great Britain on 'The South Western Limited' railtour of 18th September 1960. Working the Ascot to Eastleigh portion, the engine has been caught by Bill before/after the 'special' at Nine Elms shed.

Opposite

London Hither Green Station 34084

This interesting photograph was captured by Bill in late February 1960 to the south of Hither Green station and St Mildred's Road, looking southwest along Further Green Road. Bulleid 'Battle of Britain' Pacific no. 34084 *253 Squadron*, built at Brighton in November 1948, had a mishap while working the Dover to Bricklayers Arms freight train on 20th February and was still waiting to be put back on the rails. When this took place the engine was taken to Eastleigh Works, returned to working order, and went back into service at Dover; no. 34084's residence since March 1958. This was not the first time the engine was involved in an accident, however, as on 9th December 1949, when *253 Squadron* was arriving at London Victoria station with the 'up' 'Golden Arrow', a collision with no. 34085 *501 Squadron* occurred. Both locomotives were travelling at low speed, which luckily meant that only minor injuries to passengers were reported, but the harm caused to the Pacifics, coaching stock and track was extensive. No. 34084 sustained buckled frames, a fractured left-hand cylinder and boiler damage. *253 Squadron* was in service until October 1965 when withdrawn from Eastleigh.

Above

London Victoria Station 31033

In the late 1850s the G.W.R., L.N.W.R., L.C.&D.R. and L.B.&S.C.R. entered into an agreement to construct a terminus in Westminster after extending existing lines from Battersea. The first stage was completed in 1860 when the L.B.&S.C.R. station, on the west side of the land at the western end of Victoria Street, was opened for traffic on 1st October. From 3rd December the L.C.&D.R. facilities were operational, these being shared with the G.W.R. and on the eastern side of the site. Running light engine on this side of London Victoria station during the late 1950s is Wainwright 'C' Class 0-6-0 no. 31033. The locomotive was constructed at Ashford Works in October 1900 and was in traffic until March 1960. No. 31033 spent the 1950s working in the London area with allocations at; Bricklayers Arms (August 1950 to May 1951) Hither Green (May 1951 to May 1959), Nine Elms (May to July 1959) and Feltham (July 1959 to March 1960).

Opposite

London Nine Elms Shed 30795

Photographed being moved by Nine Elms Shed's turntable on 17th September 1960 is Maunsell 'King Arthur' no. 30795 *Sir Dinadan*. The locomotive, which was built at Eastleigh Works in April 1926, would perform just under two more years' worth of work before being condemned for scrap.

Above

Lyme Regis Station 30584

Adams '415' Class 4-4-2T locomotive no. 30584 rests at Lyme Regis station during April 1958. The latter was opened upon the completion of the branch line from Axminster on 24th August 1903. The line had been constructed under the Light Railway Act and was funded by shareholders and the L.&S.W.R., which provided approx. half of the money and agreed to run the services. The company had been involved with plans to build a line some 30 years earlier, but had been discouraged by the difficult nature of the land to the coast. This problem impacted on the successful scheme by forcing the station to be a distance from the town centre. Modest facilities were supplied; a single platform on the 'up' side hosted the trains and four sidings received any goods. A bay platform was subsequently added, along with a extensions to the station building and the platform. After closure, with the line, the station building was dismantled in the late 1970s and re-built at Alresford on the 'Watercress' line.

Below
Lyme Regis Shed 30584
No. 30584 has also been caught by Bill outside Lyme Regis shed. The '415s' working the branch were allocated to Exmouth Junction while working for B.R., but one could often be found off duty in Lyme Regis shed. This had been constructed in 1903 and was placed just to the north of the station on the east side of the line. However, a replacement was necessary only ten years later as the result of a fire consuming the timber building. The new structure was made from corrugated asbestos sheeting and proved much more durable than the previous building, being closed by B.R. in 1965. No. 30584 was condemned in early 1961 after 75 years in traffic.

Below
Lymington Pier 30111
The Lymington branch leaves the line between Southampton and Bournemouth just to the south of Brockenhurst station. Construction of this route was carried out in the late 1850s and was open for traffic to Lymington Town station from July 1858. In the early 1880s the L.&S.W.R. decided to extend the line to the south in order to provide a new service for a pier in deeper water and the resultant Lymington Pier station was opened on 1st May 1884. Drummond 'M7' no. 30111 waits impatiently at the station with a service to Brockenhurst. The engine was erected at Nine Elms in March 1904 and was in service until January 1964.

Above

Paddock Wood Station 31520

The 'H' Class design was one of two produced for local passenger work, predominantly around London, and was ultimately chosen for construction because of a wide route availability. The two cylinders were 18 in. by 26 in. with 'C' Class motion, while the boiler was 4 ft 3 in. diameter working at 160 psi. The coupled wheels were 5 ft 6 in. diameter and the trailing wheels 3 ft 7 in. diameter. Wainwright 'H' no. 31520 is seen at Paddock Wood station with a Hawkhurst-bound service in early 1961. Paddock Wood station was opened by the S.E.R. on 31st August 1842 as Maidstone Road, but renaming was carried out a short time later in 1844.

Above

Redhill Shed 31247

Stored at the rear of Redhill's three-track shed in March 1961 was Wainwright 'D' Class 4-4-0 no. 31247. The locomotive was one of ten built by Dübs & Co. in 1903, being completed in April and starting work at Dover. The livery at this time would have been green with a number of polished brass fittings, copper capped chimney and brass cab side numerals giving rise to the sobriquet 'coppertops' for the class. No. 31247 was later one of ten dispatched to Beyer, Peacock & Co. in 1921 to be rebuilt to Maunsell's 'D1' specifications, which included alterations to the cylinders, boiler and cab, the engine returning to work at Longhedge in April. At Nationalisation no. 31247 was allocated to Stewarts Lane and later had spells at Dover, Faversham, Guildford, Bricklayers Arms and Nine Elms. This latter was the official home of the engine when the picture was taken and withdrawal would soon occur in July.

Oppoosite

Redhill Shed 30914

Under preparation for the next 'turn' at Redhill, on an adjacent track to no. 31811, was 'Schools' Class no. 30914 *Eastbourne*. Underneath the thick accumulation of grime the locomotive had B.R. mixed traffic black livery applied and had been decorated in this since May 1950. But, no. 30914 was one of four 'Schools' that would end their careers without receiving the B.R. Brunswick green livery and lining. The locomotive did have Automatic Warning System apparatus fitted by B.R. in April 1959 and was in the majority on this occasion, although 17 remained without the equipment upon their withdrawal. *Eastbourne* was based at Redhill shed at the time of this picture and this was the case from April 1960 to July 1961, at which time the engine was sent for scrap.

Above

Rowfant Station 31306

No. 31306 has been photographed a short distance away from Rowfant station, which can be seen in the background, with a service from Three Bridges to East Grinstead. Rowfant was one of two stations on the branch line between the two places, the other being Grange Road. However, the former was built away from any local population and mainly served a local landowner, having just one platform originally. Another was added subsequently, along with another track to allow trains to pass each other. Rowfant also later possessed a large goods yard with oil tanks, which would have been located on the far left of this view; the line laid parallel to the running line was a siding used for trains entering and exiting the yard. The station closed with the route on 2nd January 1967.

Opposite

Redhill Shed 31811

The depot at Redhill was sited to the south of the station at the point where the Brighton route split with the Tonbridge line, also being to the north of the Redhill avoiding, or 'Quarry' line. The ramped coal stage was on the western perimeter, next to the Brighton tracks. The former was installed in 1928 along with a new 65 ft turntable, the cost of both being nearly £13,000. The tender of Maunsell 'N' Class 2-6-0 no. 31811 is being topped up in preparation for the next service in March 1961. Constructed in June 1920, the locomotive was the first of the class to be finished at Ashford after the end of World War One. Carrying out 45 years' of work, no. 31811 was condemned at Guildford in July 1965 after six years at the shed.

Above

Salisbury Station 34038

'The East Midlander' railtour was organised for 9th May 1964 by the Midland Branch of the Railway Correspondence and Travel Society and was transported from Nottingham Victoria station to Didcot behind Stanier 'Coronation' Class Pacific no. 46251 *City of Nottingham*. Bulleid 'West Country' Light Pacific no. 34038 *Lynton* then took the train of 12 carriages on a jaunt around the Southern Region before dropping the party at Swindon for the return to Nottingham with no. 46251. The itinerary on S.R. metals included stops at Newbury, Eastleigh (where the party toured the works), Salisbury and Westbury. While *Lynton* made a mid-afternoon stop at Salisbury for replenishment, a number of the travellers alighted to record the finely turned-out locomotive. No. 34038 would continue in service until June 1966.

Opposite

Salisbury Shed 30064 and 30072

Nos 30064 and 30072, 'U.S.A.' Class 0-6-0T locomotives, are pictured in Salisbury shed's yard on 4th August 1967. No. 30064 was the other member of the class, while not in departmental stock, to receive malachite green livery and this had been applied in February 1964. The engine was allocated to Eastleigh after being released from Southampton Docks in May 1963 and was condemned at the former in July 1967. No. 30072 was withdrawn in the same month after working at Guildford from February 1963 as the shed's shunting locomotive. Both class members were soon acquired by preservation societies. No. 30064 found a home on the Bluebell Railway, while no. 30072 travelled to the Keighley & Worth Valley Railway. The two locomotives are currently in need of heavy overhauls.

Above
Shepherdswell 31065
Dating from 3rd May 1960, this photograph shows no. 31065 taking on water in the area around Shepherdswell and Shepherds Well stations. The locomotive originally belonged to James Stirling's 'O' Class, being constructed in September 1896, but was rebuilt 12 years later by Wainwright to 'O1' Class specifications. No. 31065 was the last of the class to be withdrawn from traffic in July 1961 and was subsequently saved from being sent to the scrapyard.

Above

Southampton Docks Shed 30062

Facilities for locomotives working in the busy dockyards at Southampton were installed by the Southampton Docks Railway in 1865. The company converted the building previously used by horses, which had been made redundant by the steam engines, but a short time later the S.D.R. constructed a new two-track shed with gable roof. The S.R. carried out the next improvements during the 1930s as the addition of a new track on the north side saw the space between the building and the Marine Engineering Works occupied. Apart from work to the roof in the mid-1950s, the shed remained largely unaltered until closure in January 1966; diesel locomotives had use of the facilities from 1963. Steam is still in residence during March 1961 as 'U.S.A.' Class locomotives stand outside the entrance, which was on the west side of the shed. No. 30062 was constructed at Vulcan Iron Works, Wilkes-Barre, Pennsylvania, in 1942 and entered service for the S.R. in May 1947. Working from Southampton until December 1962, the locomotive was subsequently transferred to departmental stock, being renumbered DS234, and sent to Meldon Quarry, Okehampton, where employment was found until August 1966. DS234 was condemned in March 1967.

Opposite

Sidmouth Junction 30796

Heading an Exeter to Shrewsbury passenger service through Sidmouth Junction station is Maunsell 'King Arthur' no. 30796 *Sir Dodinas le Savage*.

Above

Southampton Docks Sidings 32694

Locomotive no. 32694 was constructed for the L.B.&S.C.R. in April 1875 to the design of William Stroudley, who had been with the company since 1870. The engine entered traffic as L.B.&S.C.R. no. 102 *Cherbourg* and was one of the earliest members of Stroudley's 'E' Class 0-6-0T to be completed as erection of the first had only taken place in November of the previous year. The design continued to be perpetuated until 1891, with Stroudley's successor R.J. Billinton producing a small number with detail alterations, when 80 were at work for the L.B.&S.C.R. Before grouping the locomotive's number had been changed to no. 694 and the name was also later removed.

Opposite

Southampton Docks 30068

When the New Dock at Southampton was opened in 1934, the provision of ash pits, water columns, coal stage and turntable for locomotives working on the new site was carried out by the S.R. These were located at the west end of the docks between Herbert Walker Avenue and West Bay Road. This evocative picture of 'U.S.A.' Class locomotive no. 30068 taking on water was captured in early March 1961. The capacity of the side tanks was 1,000 gallons, while the bunker could carry 1 ton 6 cwt of coal. The engine is displaying the Southampton Docks shed code, '71I'. This would become '70I' from September 1963, but no. 30068 would not carry this as a transfer to Eastleigh occurred in June of that year. Allocation to the depot would be brief as withdrawal transpired in March 1964, with the engine becoming the second class member to be scrapped by B.R.

Above

Southampton Docks Sidings 30070

After the end of the Second World War the motive power working the docks at Southampton were in need of heavy, and expensive, repair work. As a number of designs had been erected for the military, and now surplus to requirements, Bulleid turned to a class of 0-6-0T locomotives built for the American Army to handle the dock traffic. A total of 14 were bought; thirteen were constructed by Vulcan Iron Works and two by H.K. Porter, Inc. Only one of these latter were taken into service, however, as the other was used for spare parts. The locomotives were added to stock between May 1946 and November 1947, with War Department no. 1960 becoming S.R. no. 70 in April of the latter year. After entering service, the class were slightly modified to have ventilators on the cab roof, rectangular instead of circular front lookout windows and extended coal bunkers. These were applied to no. 30070 in January 1948. In the mid-1950s radio communication equipment was also fitted so crews could be quickly directed to necessary work. Evidently there was a lull in traffic when this picture was taken allowing all concerned to take a break.

Opposite

Southampton Docks Sidings 32694

Another view, with the South Western Hotel in the background, of no. 32694 shunting goods in Southampton Docks sidings during March 1961. Only 50 of the 80 'E' Class engines, later 'E1', were taken into stock by B.R. (the first class member was scrapped in 1908) and the numbers reduced quickly as the 1950s progressed. No. 32694 has the distinction of being the last 'E1' to be condemned, this happening in July 1961 after several moves between Fratton shed and Southampton Docks while serving under B.R. The latter hosted no. 32694 for the final time and saw the locomotive's 86 years of service come to an end. Eastleigh Works broke up no. 32694 shortly afterwards.

Above

Swanage Station 30105

'M7' Class locomotive no. 30105 has been photographed waiting to return home with a service from Swanage station. The engine was Bournemouth-allocated from June 1951 to withdrawal in April 1963.

Opposite

Three Bridges Shed 32342

Billinton's 'K' Class had a history of being used to test the merits of new or different equipment and no. 32342 was one locomotive to feature in such trials. In March 1922 the engine was fitted with a Kylälä variable blastpipe, along with classmate no. 341 and 'B4' no. 44. From the date of fitting to June, the 'K' Class engines underwent a series of assessments with 61 and 64-wagon trains. Both engines demonstrated an economy, in terms of coal saved per train mile, with the Kylälä apparatus against the standard chimney arrangement when tested against each other. However, a discrepancy emerged when the locomotives performed the duties against themselves. No. 32342, with a heavier train, used less coal with the normal blastpipe, whereas no. 341 saved nearly 8% of coal with the Kylälä blastpipe. The 'B4' showed a small saving with the latter type, but not enough to warrant persisting with and was later discarded. Interestingly, the Kylälä equipment was later developed by eminent French locomotive engineer André Chapelon into the 'Kylchap' double blastpipe chimney, which found extensive use on the continent and England in the locomotives of Sir Nigel Gresley. No. 32342, which was withdrawn in December 1962 from Brighton, is seen on Three Bridges shed's turntable in March 1961.

Below

Three Bridges Station 31306

Wainwright 'H' locomotive no. 31306 is ready to take a passenger train from Three Bridges to East Grinstead during March 1961. Constructed in May 1906, as the second class member to be completed in the year, the majority of the locomotive's career was spent without 'push and pull' apparatus. This was fitted in November 1959 and a number of other 'H' engines were late recipients, the last being no. 31324 in January 1961. In fact, the decision to equip any 'H' 0-4-4T was only made after Nationalisation, due to the withdrawal of older classes fitted with 'push and pull' equipment. No. 31306's final allocation was to Three Bridges shed; this began in May 1960 and lasted until December 1961. The engine had spent time at Ashford, Dover, Gillingham and Bricklayers Arms while under B.R. employment.

Above

Three Bridges Station 31551

Another view taken at Three Bridges station, but the date in this instance is 24th June 1962. A 'H' Class engine is again featured, no. 31551 being slightly older than no. 31306 after entering service from Ashford in January 1905. The locomotive is also with an East Grinstead service. People from the town had come together in the early 1850s to promote a railway to the L.B.&S.C.R. line at Three Bridges, opened on 12th July 1841, approx. seven miles away to the west. The scheme progressed quickly and the line was opened on 9th July 1855. No. 31551 was condemned at Three Bridges depot in January 1964.

Above

Tonbridge Station 31877

The 'N1' Class were a development of Maunsell's 'N' Class 2-6-0s through the use of three cylinders. The prototype, no. 822, was completed at Ashford in March 1923, but a further five 'N1s' did not appear until 1930. No. 31877 was released into traffic during April, being initially allocated to New Cross. After Nationalisation the engine was based at Hither Green with the other five 'N1's and was later removed to Tonbridge in May 1959 as a result of the Kent electrification scheme. No. 31877 rounds the curve off the Tonbridge 'cut-off' line, past Wainwright 'C' no. 31579, into the town's station.

Opposite

Tonbridge Shed 31684

'C' Class 0-6-0 no. 31684 had two residencies at Tonbridge depot under B.R. The first occurred in the early 1950s to August 1951, while the second started in October 1959 and lasted until withdrawal in October 1961.

Previous Page

Tonbridge Shed 31771

Wainwright 'L' Class 4-4-0 no. 31771 is pictured at Tonbridge during the final part of an allocation to the shed, which comprised the period September 1952 to May 1959. At the latter date the engine was moved to Nine Elms and no. 31771's career ended at the depot in November 1961.

Tonbridge Shed 31857

Entering service in April 1925, Maunsell 'N' Class 2-6-0 no. 31857 was in traffic until January 1964. The engine was perhaps working from Hither Green when pictured at Tonbridge; this allocation lasted from July 1951 to January 1961. Feltham, Exmouth Junction and Guildford would subsequently house the locomotive.

Tonbridge Shed 31766
Withdrawn from Nine Elms shed in February 1961, Wainwright 'L' no. 31766 had only spent a relatively short time at the depot, being allocated there from May 1959. The engine is seen at Tonbridge on 18th May 1962 waiting to be scrapped.

Tonbridge Shed 33034
Tonbridge-allocated 'Q1' no. 33034 was a long-term resident at the depot, along with several other class members used to work goods trains to Hastings. The 'Q1s' were a mainstay at Tonbridge for this purpose until ousted by diesels in the early 1960s; no. 33034 left in May 1961.

Tonbridge Shed 31756

Two 'L1' Class 4-4-0s were allocated to Tonbridge by B.R.; no. 31783 and the featured 31756. This comprised the period January to June 1960 both arriving, apparently on loan, from Nine Elms depot as the pair would return to the capital and later be withdrawn in November and September 1961 respectively.

Tonbridge Shed 31906
Maunsell 'U1' Class 2-6-0 no. 31906 is seen between duties at Tonbridge shed. The engine was one of a small number of 'U1s' to acquire B.R.-type blastpipes and chimney liner.

Tonbridge Shed 30379
Also 'on shed' during Bill's visit was Drummond 'M7' no. 30379.

Below
Tonbridge Shed 31266
Located to the east of the station on the south side of the
S.E.R. main line and just past the Tunbridge Wells route,
Tonbridge shed was opened by the aforementioned
company in May 1842. Originally three tracks were
provided, entering the dead-end shed on the eastern
side, but later another three-road through building
was constructed on the southern side. A coal stage
and 55 ft turntable were also additions at this time.
The former was located on the western side of the shed
in close proximity with the running lines. Taking on
water and having the ashes removed at the shed is 'H'
Class locomotive no. 31266, which was working from
Tunbridge Wells at the time.

Above

Tonbridge Station 30932

Approaching Tonbridge station from the west on the Tonbridge 'cut-off' line is no. 30932 *Blundell's*. Seen in the distance is Tonbridge 'A' signal box and to the left of this, out of view, was the track leading to Redhill. A feature present behind the signal box, which would be replaced in 1962 by a power box, is Tonbridge West yard, opened in 1941 and still active. No. 30932 was erected in January 1935 and was paired with tender no. 732. In 1938, Bulleid had this modified to incorporate higher side sheets and angled bunker floor so that coal would slip forward as that at the front was shovelled out. The tender was the only one running behind a 'Schools' locomotive altered, but was later switched, in August 1958, with tender no. 705 from no. 30905 *Tonbridge* and this is the one seen here with *Blundell's*.

Above

Tonbridge Station 31177

Originally the S.E.R. opened Tonbridge station on the eastern side of the road bridge, which is out of sight on the right behind the station building and footbridge over the lines, in May 1842. With the installation of the Tonbridge 'cut-off' line, new facilities were opened on the western side of the road bridge and timber construction for the station buildings was discarded in favour of brick. The S.R. completely rebuilt the latter and the platforms, which were extended in length to the west, in 1935 and the footbridge was also an addition at this time. 'H' Class locomotive no. 31177 is photographed at the 'down' platform with a service to Hawkhurst.

Below

Tonbridge 32578

Seemingly abandoned to the elements at Tonbridge is Billinton 'E4' Class 0-6-2T no. 32578. The locomotive is adorned, partially, with B.R. mixed traffic black, but when sent into traffic in June 1903 a more cheerful scheme was used. Stroudley passenger yellow was applied to the engine, as L.B.&S.C.R. no. 578 *Horsebridge*, and this was used on the majority of the 75 class members, which were constructed between 1897 and 1903. A small number were decorated in Stroudley green, but by the end of 1910 nearly all had been repainted in a new Umber livery and the names bestowed on the engines were removed. A further colour change occurred upon Grouping as S.R. green was chosen for the 'E4s'. At this time no. S2578 was allocated to Coulsden; by Nationalisation a move to Bricklayers Arms had transpired. No. 32578 then spent much of the 1950s working from Tonbridge, with a short spell at St Leonards at the end of 1954, and left for Brighton in August 1960. The locomotive was taken out of service in April 1961.

Below
Tonbridge Station 31902
After the reconstruction of the three-cylinder 'K1' Class 2-6-4T locomotive no. A890 *River Frome* into a 2-6-0 tender engine, the decision was made to construct twenty new locomotives with similar specifications. The main difference was that the new engines, classified 'U1', would have three sets of Walschaerts valve gear whereas *River Frome* had two sets with Holcroft conjugated motion driving the valve for the centre cylinder. A larger tender was also provided with 4,000 gallon capacity, instead of 3,500 gallons, but the same amount of coal could be carried - 5 tons. No. 31902 was a product of Eastleigh Works in July 1931 and went new to Hastings but soon moved to Stewarts Lane. The engine was working from Bricklayers Arms when this photograph was captured at Tonbridge's 'down' platform. London's Norwood Junction depot would see the engine condemned in November 1962.

Above

Tonbridge Station 31850

A number of names were used for Tonbridge station in the latter half of the nineteenth century. Initially Tunbridge was applied, but in the early 1850s Tunbridge Junction became the title after the line to Hastings was completed. Before the start of the 1900s the present spelling had been adopted, but Junction was not removed until the late 1920s. Also seen at the station's 'down' platform is 'N' Class engine no. 31850. The former's canopy, extending 400 feet, was slightly longer than the one on the 'up' side, which was just over 360 ft in length.

Wenford 30585

Looking southwards at Wenford china clay dries and L.&S.W.R. Beattie '0298' Class 2-4-0WT no. 30585 is seen with a train of empty wagons. Impressively, the locomotive, and two other class mates, spent approximately 65 years working in the area handling the china clay traffic, in addition to granite from a local quarry, on the minerals branch from Bodmin to Wenfordbridge. The Bodmin and Wadebridge Railway opened the

line in October 1834 and the traffic ran until the early 1980s. No. 30585 was built by Beyer, Peacock & Co. in May 1874 and was withdrawn in December 1962. The engine was subsequently stopped from being sent to the scrapyard by the London Railway Preservation Society and found a home at the Buckinghamshire Railway Centre. The locomotive is currently at work, having undergone a full restoration in the early 2000s.

Below

Wadebridge Station 30586

Posing for Bill's camera at the eastern end of Wadebridge station is another Beattie '0298' Class engine, no. 30586. The class were altered from their original design, which was produced for the passenger traffic in and out of the suburbs around London. No cab was provided when built and these were added to survivors in the 1890s when a new Adams boiler was also fitted; later a Drummond-type boiler was used. No. 30586 was unusual from the other two class members in having square splashers over the driving wheels, rather than round ones. Wadebridge shed, which was located on the opposite side of the station (the water tank is visible behind the engine's bunker), housed the class upon their arrival in the late 1890s until they were all removed in December 1962. No. 30586 was the only one to be sent to be cut-up as no. 30587 was taken into the National Collection. The latter is presently located close to engines' former workplace on the Bodmin & Wenford Railway.

Above

Westerham Station 31177

No. 31177 was constructed at Ashford Works in March 1909 and worked initially from Bricklayers Arms. During the Second World War the locomotive was one of three 'Hs' loaned to the London, Midland & Scottish Railway, which dispatched the engines to Forfar to work the local service to Arbroath; no. 1177 returned to the S.R. in mid-1944. Stewarts Lane depot had possession of the locomotive at Nationalisation, then in April 1951 no. 31177 was dispatched to Tonbridge and this allocation would continue until the engine was condemned in September 1961. The picture has been taken from the embankment past the signal box at Westerham station (platform side) looking east.

Below
Wadebridge Shed 30586
No. 30586 has also been pictured in Wadebridge shed's yard. Two depots were used by locomotives during the years of steam traction. The first was located on the northern edge of the station on the west side of the running lines and was completed by the B.&W.R. with their route. The second was erected in 1895 on the west side of the station, superseding the first, which remained standing for a number of years subsequently. The coal stage can be seen behind no. 30586, while the 50 ft turntable was located to the north (left) a slight distance away from the shed. As well as the Beattie engines, the shed's allocation consisted of Adams 'O2' Class locomotives, but in the early 1960s a number of Western Region 0-6-0PT and B.R. Standard Class 2 2-6-2T were rostered to Wadebridge.

Above

Westerham Station 31533

No. 31533 is seen from the same vantage point at Westerham station as no. 31177. The two engines' class mate no. 31518 was involved in a celebration of the line's service to the local community before closure. Trains on the 28th October were worked by the engine in the morning, then in the afternoon 'D1' no. 31739 and 'Q1' no. 33029 alternated taking passengers between Dunton Green and Westerham. After the branch closed an attempt was made to purchase the line but this came to no avail and much of the route has since been enveloped by the M25 motorway.

Above
Westerham Station 31177

Wainwright 'H' Class engine no. 31177 has arrived at Westerham station with a service from Dunton Green. The former station dated from the 7th July 1881 and was the terminus for a four-and-a-half mile long branch from the latter station on the Tonbridge 'cut-off' line. Two other stations were on the route and these were Brasted and Chevening Halt, although the latter was not opened until the early 20th century. Westerham station consisted of a single platform and run-around loop, which is the line seen on the right of the engine. On the extreme right of the picture is the track to the station's goods shed. The branch was closed by B.R. on 30th October 1961.

Opposite
Yeovil Junction Station 30131

Drummond 'M7' no. 30131 seems eager to depart from Yeovil Junction station's 'up' platform with a service to Yeovil Town station during August 1961. The former station was opened by the L.&S.W.R. on 19th July 1860 after the completion of the final section of the company's line to Exeter from London. Yeovil Town, which was nearer the centre of the populace, was ready for traffic slightly later on 1st June 1861, but was a replacement for an earlier station belonging to the Bristol & Exeter Railway. On the Castle Cary to Weymouth line, Yeovil Pen Mill also served the town from the mid-1850s. No. 30131 was amongst the final five members of the 'M7' Class, which totalled 105, to be completed in 1911. Eastleigh Works sent the engine into traffic during November of that year after taking the reins of locomotive construction from Nine Elms in 1909. In all, ten 'M7s' were erected on the south coast. The locomotive was working in the area at the start of 1948 from Bournemouth depot and would remain there until September 1951. At this time the engine was taken on to the books at Yeovil Town shed and continued to be on the roster there until condemned in November 1962. Yeovil Town station was closed in October 1966, while Yeovil Junction was subsequently heavily modified, this including the 'down' platform being taken out of use, shortening of the footbridge (seen on the left), and reduction in the number of running lines.

Bibliography

Bradley, D.L. *Locomotives of the L.B.&S.C.R. Part Three.* 1974.

Bradley, D.L. *The Locomotive History of the London, Chatham & Dover Railway.* 1979.

Bradley, D.L. *The Locomotives of the South Eastern Railway.* 1963.

Bradley, D.L. *The Locomotives of the Southern Railway Part One.* 1975.

Bradley, D.L. *The Locomotives of the Southern Railway Part Two.* 1976.

Bradley, D.L. *The Locomotives of the South Eastern & Chatham Railway.* 1961.

Griffiths, Roger and Paul Smith. *The Directory of British Engine Sheds and Principal Locomotive Servicing Points: 1 Southern England, the Midlands, East Anglia and Wales.* 1999.

Hawkins, Chris and George Reeve. *An Historical Survey of Southern Sheds.* 2001.

Quick, Michael. *Railway Passenger Stations in Great Britain: A Chronology.* 2009.

R.C.T.S. *The Locomotives of the Great Western Railway Part Five: Six-Coupled Tank Engines.* 1958.

Swift, Peter. *Locomotives in Detail 6: Maunsell 4-4-0 Schools Class.* 2006.

Walmsley, Tony. *Shed by Shed Part Five: Southern.* 2008.